Emotional Intelligence and Self-Regulation for Kids Ages 6-10

Strategies for Helping Kids Manage Stress and Emotions

BY
DALTON WYMAN

CONTENTS

INTRODUCTION

Welcome aboard, young explorers! Today marks the beginning of an exciting journey into the world of emotions and self-regulation. Buckle up as we embark on a thrilling adventure towards understanding ourselves better and learning valuable skills that will help us navigate through life's ups and downs.

Understanding Emotional Intelligence

First things first, let's talk about emotional intelligence. You might be wondering, what exactly is emotional intelligence? Well, it's like having a superpower that helps you understand and manage your own emotions, as well as understand and relate to the feelings of others. Just imagine being able to identify what you're feeling and why you're feeling that way. Pretty cool, right?

Now, you might be thinking, why is emotional intelligence important for kids like us? That's a great question! Emotional intelligence is like a secret weapon that can help us in so many ways. It helps us build stronger relationships with friends and family, handle tough situations with grace, and even perform better in school. So, by learning about emotional intelligence, we're basically unlocking the key to becoming superheroes of our own emotions!

Emotional intelligence is made up of several key components, including:

- Self-awareness: This means being aware of our own emotions and understanding why we feel the way we do. For example, if we're feeling angry, self-awareness helps us recognize that anger and understand what might have triggered it.

- Self-regulation: This involves managing our emotions in healthy ways. Instead of letting our emotions control us, self-regulation helps us stay calm and in control, even when things get tough.

- Empathy: Empathy is the ability to understand and share the feelings of others. It's like stepping into someone else's shoes and seeing the world from their perspective. By being empathetic, we can build stronger connections with the people around us and show kindness and compassion.

- Social skills: These are the skills we use to interact with others, such as communication, teamwork, and conflict resolution. Good social skills help us build positive relationships and navigate social situations with ease.

What to Expect in This Book

Alright, let's take a quick peek at what's in store for us in this book. Get ready for some action-packed chapters filled with fun activities, helpful tips, and inspiring stories. We'll dive deep into different emotions, learn how to express ourselves in healthy ways, and discover effective strategies for managing stress and tough situations.

But wait, there's more! We'll also explore the fascinating world of self-regulation. Now, you might be wondering, what's self-regulation? Well, it's all about being able to control our thoughts, feelings, and actions, even when things get tough. Think of it as having a powerful remote control that helps us stay calm and focused, no matter what's happening around us.

In this book, we'll cover topics such as:

- Understanding our emotions: We'll learn about different emotions and how they affect us, as well as strategies for managing them in healthy ways.

- Expressing ourselves: We'll explore different ways to express our emotions, from talking about them to using creative outlets like art and music.

- Building resilience: We'll discover how to bounce back from setbacks and develop the resilience to overcome challenges with confidence.

- Practicing self-care: We'll learn the importance of taking care of ourselves, both physically and emotionally, and explore ways to practice self-care in our daily lives.

- Developing social skills: We'll dive into the world of social skills and learn how to communicate effectively, make friends, and navigate social situations with ease.

- Cultivating mindfulness: We'll explore the practice of mindfulness and how it can help us stay present, calm our minds, and reduce stress.

Joining Forces: Kids and Parents

Hey, parents! This journey isn't just for us kids. We need your help too! Together, we can tackle these challenges and emerge victorious. So, let's team up and work through the exercises and activities in this book. Your support and guidance mean the world to us, and we couldn't do it without you!

Parents, you play a crucial role in helping us develop emotional intelligence and self-regulation skills. By modeling healthy emotional expression and providing a safe and supportive environment for us to explore our feelings, you're laying the foundation for a lifetime of emotional well-being. So, thank you for being our partners on this journey!

The Power of Patience and Practice

Before we dive into the exciting world of emotions and self-regulation, there's one more thing we need to talk about: patience and practice. Learning new skills takes time and effort, so let's remember to be patient with ourselves and each other. And don't forget, practice makes perfect! The more we practice these skills, the stronger we'll become.

As we journey through this book together, let's keep an open mind and a positive attitude. Let's celebrate our successes, learn from our mistakes, and support each other every step of the way. With patience, practice, and perseverance, we can unlock the incredible power of emotional intelligence and self-regulation.

So, are you ready to embark on this incredible journey together? Grab your capes, put on your thinking caps, and let's dive into the world of emotional intelligence and self-regulation!

Chapter 01

Understanding Emotions

Welcome to the colorful world of emotions! In this chapter, we'll dive deep into the ocean of feelings, exploring the different colors and shades that make up our emotional landscape. Get ready to embark on an exciting journey as we learn to understand, recognize, and embrace our emotions.

Exploring Basic Emotions

Emotions are like the colors of a rainbow—vibrant, diverse, and constantly changing. At the heart of our emotional palette are five basic emotions: happiness, sadness, anger, fear, and excitement. Let's take a closer look at each one:

- Happy: When something brings us joy or makes us smile, we're experiencing happiness. It's like sunshine warming our hearts on a bright summer day.
- Sad: Sadness comes over us when we feel hurt, disappointed, or lonely. It's like a rainy day when the sky is gray and tears fall like raindrops.
- Angry: Anger flares up when we feel frustrated, irritated, or unfairly treated. It's like a storm brewing inside us, with thunder rumbling and lightning flashing.
- Scared: Fear creeps in when we encounter something unfamiliar or threatening. It's like shadows lurking in the dark, making us want to hide or run away.
- Excited: Excitement fills us with anticipation and energy when something fun or thrilling is about to happen. It's like fireworks exploding in the night sky, lighting up our world with sparks of joy.

Visualizing Emotions

To help us better understand emotions, let's turn to the power of visuals. Imagine a colorful palette of emotions, each one represented by a different facial expression. When we're happy, our eyes sparkle, and our lips curve into a big, bright smile. When we're sad, our brows furrow, and tears well up in our eyes. And when we're angry, our jaw clenches, and our fists may tighten in frustration.

Colorful Illustrations

To bring these emotions to life, let's use colorful illustrations that capture the essence of each feeling. Picture a happy face with a wide grin and twinkling eyes, a sad face with drooping shoulders and teardrops, an angry face with furrowed brows and a scowling mouth, a scared face with wide eyes and trembling lips, and an excited face with raised eyebrows and a beaming expression.

Identifying Emotions

Now that we've learned about the different emotions, it's time to put our knowledge into practice. Let's create a simple emotion chart to help kids identify how they feel. This chart can feature colorful emojis or faces representing each emotion, along with space for kids to write or draw about their own feelings.

Emotion Chart Activity

Every day, kids can check in with themselves and fill out their emotion chart. They can reflect on how they're feeling in the moment and choose the emoji or face that best matches their emotions. Are they feeling happy, sad, angry, scared, excited, or maybe a combination of different feelings? By regularly tracking their emotions, kids can become more aware of their emotional patterns and learn to express themselves more effectively.

Embracing All Emotions

It's important for kids to understand that all emotions are normal and okay. Just like the colors of a rainbow, each emotion serves a purpose and adds richness to our lives. Whether we're feeling happy, sad, angry, scared, or excited, it's okay to embrace our feelings and express ourselves authentically.

Emotion Diary Activity

To further explore their emotions, kids can create an "emotion diary" to track their daily feelings. They can jot down or draw about different situations that made them feel a certain way and reflect on how they responded to those emotions. Did they laugh with friends, cry over a sad movie, get angry at a sibling, feel scared during a thunderstorm, or get excited about a upcoming event? By writing or drawing about their experiences, kids can gain valuable insights into their emotional world.

Naming Emotions Through Stories and Role-Playing

To reinforce their understanding of emotions, kids can engage in storytelling and role-playing activities. They can take turns telling stories about characters experiencing different emotions and discuss how they would react in similar situations. They can also role-play scenarios where they act out various emotions and practice expressing themselves in healthy ways.

Storytelling Session

Gather around and let's spin some tales about emotions! Imagine a brave knight feeling excited as he embarks on a quest to rescue a princess. Or a sad puppy feeling lonely until he finds a new friend to play with. By weaving stories about emotions, kids can learn to empathize with others and understand the impact of their feelings on themselves and those around them.

Role-Playing Adventure

Now, it's time to put on our imaginary hats and step into the shoes of different characters. Let's pretend to be a happy explorer discovering a hidden treasure, an angry dragon breathing fire, or a scared astronaut floating in space. Through role-playing, kids can experiment with different emotions in a safe and supportive environment, building empathy, confidence, and emotional resilience along the way.

Conclusion

As we wrap up our journey through the colorful world of emotions, remember that understanding, recognizing, and embracing our feelings is an ongoing adventure. By exploring the spectrum of emotions, using visuals to visualize our feelings, identifying emotions through charts and diaries, and practicing naming emotions through storytelling and role-playing, kids can develop a deeper sense of self-awareness, empathy, and emotional intelligence. So, let's continue to sail the seas of emotions with curiosity, compassion, and courage, knowing that each wave brings new opportunities for growth and discovery.

Chapter 02

Recognizing Stress

Welcome to Chapter 2 of our adventure: Recognizing Stress! In this chapter, we'll embark on a journey to understand what stress is, how it affects us, and most importantly, how we can manage it. So, let's dive in and explore the world of stress together!

Understanding Stress

Imagine you're standing in the middle of a busy city street with cars honking, people rushing past, and loud noises everywhere — that's how it feels when we're stressed. Stress is like a big pile of rocks weighing down on our shoulders, making us feel overwhelmed, anxious, or tense. It's our body's way of reacting to challenges or changes in our environment.

What Causes Stress?

For kids, there are many things that can cause stress. It could be the pressure of schoolwork, making new friends, or dealing with changes at home, like moving to a new house or parents getting divorced. Sometimes even fun things like birthday parties or sleepovers can be stressful because they're new or different from what we're used to.

The Stress Thermometer

Just like how a thermometer measures temperature, we can use a "stress thermometer" to gauge how stressed we're feeling. Picture a thermometer with different levels, from cool and calm to hot and bothered. By checking in with our feelings regularly, we can see where we fall on the stress scale and take steps to manage our stress levels.

Checking In with Our Feelings

Throughout the day, we can ask ourselves, "How am I feeling right now?" Are we feeling cool as a cucumber, warm like a sunny day, or hot under the collar? By becoming more aware of our emotions, we can better understand what's causing our stress and take action to address it.

Recognizing Physical Signs of Stress

Stress doesn't just affect our minds—it can also show up in our bodies. Have you ever noticed your tummy feeling queasy before a big test or your head pounding after a fight with a friend? These are all signs that our bodies are feeling stressed.

Listen to Your Body

When we're stressed, our bodies send us signals to let us know something's not quite right. It could be a stomach ache, headache, tense muscles, or even trouble sleeping. By paying attention to these physical signs, we can learn to recognize when we're feeling stressed and take steps to relax and unwind.

Relaxation Techniques

Now that we've identified what stress feels like, let's explore some simple relaxation techniques to help us chill out and find our calm.

Deep Breathing

One of the easiest ways to relax is by taking deep breaths. Imagine you're blowing up a balloon — breathe in slowly through your nose, filling your belly with air like the balloon expanding. Then, breathe out slowly through your mouth, letting all the air out like you're deflating the balloon. Repeat this a few times, and you'll feel yourself start to relax and unwind.

Creating a Stress Toolkit

Just like a superhero has their trusty utility belt, we can create our own "stress toolkit" filled with items that help us calm down when we're feeling overwhelmed.

What's in Your Toolkit?

Think about things that make you feel happy, calm, or comforted. It could be a favorite stuffed animal, a cozy blanket, a stress ball to squeeze, or a special book to read. You can also include things like calming music, coloring pages, or a journal to write down your thoughts and feelings. The important thing is to fill your toolkit with things that work for you and help you feel better when you're stressed.

Conclusion

Congratulations! You've completed Chapter 2: Recognizing Stress. We've learned what stress is, identified common stressors for kids, used a stress thermometer to gauge our stress levels, discussed physical signs of stress, introduced simple relaxation techniques like deep breathing, and created a stress toolkit filled with items to help us calm down.

By recognizing when we're feeling stressed and knowing how to manage it, we can navigate through life's ups and downs with greater ease and resilience. So, the next time you're feeling stressed, remember to check in with your feelings, take a few deep breaths, and reach for your stress toolkit. You've got this!

Chapter 03

Deep Breathing Techniques

Welcome to Chapter 3: Deep Breathing Techniques! In this chapter, we'll explore the power of deep breathing and learn how it can help us calm down and find our inner peace. So, take a deep breath and let's dive in!

The Benefits of Deep Breathing

Deep breathing isn't just for blowing out birthday candles — it's a superpower that can help us relax, reduce stress, and feel more centered. When we take slow, deep breaths, we send a signal to our brain that it's time to calm down and relax. It's like pressing the reset button on our body and mind, helping us find our balance in the midst of chaos.

How Deep Breathing Works

When we're stressed, our body goes into "fight or flight" mode, which is our natural response to danger. This causes our heart rate to increase, our muscles to tense up, and our breathing to become shallow and rapid. Deep breathing helps counteract this response by activating the "rest and digest" mode, which slows down our heart rate, relaxes our muscles, and encourages deeper, more controlled breaths.

Benefits for the Body and Mind

By practicing deep breathing regularly, we can lower our heart rate, reduce muscle tension, and quiet our racing thoughts. It's like stepping into a peaceful oasis amidst the hustle and bustle of everyday life. Whether we're feeling anxious before a big test, frustrated after a disagreement with a friend, or simply need a moment to unwind, deep breathing can be our trusted companion. Some specific benefits of deep breathing include:

- Reduced Anxiety: Deep breathing helps to calm the nervous system and reduce feelings of anxiety and panic.
- Improved Focus: By slowing down our breathing, we can increase our concentration and stay present in the moment.
- Better Sleep: Practicing deep breathing before bedtime can help us relax and fall asleep more easily.
- Enhanced Mood: Deep breathing increases the flow of oxygen to the brain, which can boost our mood and energy levels.

Belly Breathing Activity

Let's start our deep breathing journey with a fun activity using a stuffed animal. Belly breathing, also known as diaphragmatic breathing, focuses on breathing deeply into the belly rather than the chest. This type of breathing helps us to fully oxygenate our bodies and promote relaxation.

How to Do Belly Breathing

1. Find a Comfortable Position: Sit or lie down in a comfortable position. If you're lying down, place a pillow under your knees to support your lower back.
2. Place Your Stuffed Animal on Your Belly: Take your favorite stuffed animal and place it on your belly.
3. Breathe In: Slowly breathe in through your nose,

imagining that you're inflating a balloon in your belly. Watch the stuffed animal rise as your belly expands.

4. Breathe Out: Slowly breathe out through your mouth, imagining the balloon deflating. Watch the stuffed animal sink as your belly contracts.

5. Repeat: Continue this pattern of breathing for a few minutes, focusing on the rise and fall of the stuffed animal.

Fun Variations

To make belly breathing even more engaging, try these fun variations:

- Belly Breathing Buddies: Practice belly breathing with a friend or family member. Lie down next to each other and place your stuffed animals on your bellies. Watch them rise and fall in sync as you breathe together.
- Belly Breathing Race: Set a timer for one minute and see how many deep breaths you can take in that time. Challenge yourself to beat your record each day.

Balloon Breathing Visualization

Now, let's take our deep breathing to the next level with a fun visualization exercise. Balloon breathing helps us to visualize the process of filling our lungs with air and releasing it, making it easier to practice deep breathing.

How to Do Balloon Breathing

1. Close Your Eyes: Sit or lie down in a comfortable position and close your eyes.
2. Imagine a Balloon: Picture a big, colorful balloon in your hands. It can be any color you like.
3. Breathe In: Slowly breathe in through your nose, imagining that you're filling the balloon with air. Feel your lungs expand as the balloon grows bigger.
4. Breathe Out: Slowly breathe out through your mouth, imagining the air leaving the balloon. Feel your lungs contract as the balloon shrinks.
5. Repeat: Continue this pattern of breathing for a few minutes, focusing on the expansion and contraction of the balloon.

Fun Variations

To make balloon breathing more enjoyable, try these creative variations:

- Balloon Breathing Colors: Imagine that the balloon changes colors with each breath. Start with one color and see how many different colors you can visualize.
- Balloon Breathing Shapes: Instead of a round balloon, imagine different shapes like a heart, star, or animal. Picture the shape expanding and contracting with each breath.

The 4-7-8 Breathing Technique

Ready to supercharge your deep breathing skills? Introducing the 4-7-8 breathing technique! This simple yet powerful exercise can help you relax and unwind in just a few minutes. It involves inhaling for a count of 4, holding the breath for a count of 7, and exhaling for a count of 8. This technique helps to regulate the breath and activate the relaxation response.

How to Do the 4-7-8 Breathing Technique

1. Get Comfortable: Find a quiet place to sit or lie down, and close your eyes if you'd like.
2. Breathe In: Take a slow, deep breath in through your nose for a count of 4 seconds, feeling your belly rise as you fill your lungs with air.
3. Hold Your Breath: Hold your breath for a count of 7 seconds, feeling the air filling your chest and expanding your lungs.
4. Breathe Out: Slowly breathe out through your mouth for a count of 8 seconds, emptying your lungs completely and feeling any tension melting away.
5. Repeat: Continue this 4-7-8 breathing pattern for a few cycles, allowing yourself to sink deeper into relaxation with each breath.

Tips for Practicing 4-7-8 Breathing

- Start Slow: If holding your breath for 7 seconds feels challenging, start with a shorter duration and gradually increase it as you become more comfortable.
- Practice Regularly: Incorporate the 4-7-8 technique into your daily routine, such as before bedtime or during moments of stress.
- Stay Focused: Concentrate on counting and the rhythm of your breath to stay focused and present.

Using a Breathing App or Timer

Sometimes it can be helpful to use a breathing app or timer to guide your deep breathing practice. These apps often offer customizable breathing exercises, soothing music, and visualizations to help you relax and focus. Set aside a few minutes each day to practice deep breathing with your favorite app or timer, and watch as your stress melts away like snowflakes in the sun.

Recommended Breathing Apps

- Calm: Offers guided breathing exercises, relaxing music, and nature sounds to help you unwind.
- Headspace: Provides mindfulness and meditation exercises, including deep breathing techniques.
- Breathe2Relax: Designed specifically for stress management, this app guides you through deep breathing exercises with visual and audio cues.
- Using a Timer

If you prefer not to use an app, a simple timer can also be effective. Set a timer for 5-10 minutes and practice your chosen deep breathing technique during that time. Focus on your breath and allow yourself to fully relax.

Breathing Buddies Routine

Deep breathing is even more fun when you do it with a friend or family member! Create a "breathing buddies" routine where you practice deep breathing together at the same time each day. You can sit back-to-back, hold hands, or simply close your eyes and focus on your breathing together. Not only will you both benefit from the calming effects of deep breathing, but you'll also strengthen your bond and create a sense of harmony and connection.

How to Create a Breathing Buddies Routine

1. Choose a Buddy: Find a friend, sibling, or family member who wants to practice deep breathing with you.
2. Pick a Time: Decide on a specific time each day to practice deep breathing together. It could be in the morning, after school, or before bedtime.
3. Get Comfortable: Find a quiet place where you can sit or lie down comfortably.
4. Choose a Technique: Decide which deep breathing technique you want to practice, such as belly breathing, balloon breathing, or the 4-7-8 technique.
5. Practice Together: Follow the steps of your chosen technique, focusing on your breath and the presence of your buddy.

Fun Variations

- Breathing Games: Turn your deep breathing practice into a game. For example, see who can hold their breath the longest or who can blow up an imaginary balloon the biggest.
- Breathing Stories: Create a story together where you use deep breathing to help the characters relax and solve problems. Take turns adding to the story with each breath.

Conclusion

Congratulations! You've completed Chapter 3: Deep Breathing Techniques. We've explored the benefits of deep breathing for calming down, introduced belly breathing and balloon breathing activities, learned the 4-7-8 breathing technique, discussed using a breathing app or timer for regular practice, and created a breathing buddies routine with a friend or family member.

By incorporating deep breathing into your daily routine, you can cultivate a sense of calm, balance, and resilience that will serve you well in any situation. So, keep practicing your deep breathing techniques, and remember that your breath is always there to anchor you in the present moment, no matter what storms may arise. Happy breathing!

Chapter 04
Positive Self-Talk

Welcome to Chapter 4: Positive Self-Talk! In this chapter, we'll discover the incredible power of the words we say to ourselves and how they can shape our thoughts, feelings, and actions. Get ready to unlock the magic of positive self-talk and cultivate a mindset filled with optimism, confidence, and self-love.

Understanding Self-Talk

Have you ever noticed the little voice inside your head that chatters away all day long? That's your self-talk! Self-talk is the way we speak to ourselves in our minds, whether it's consciously or unconsciously. It's like having a conversation with our inner cheerleader or our inner critic. And believe it or not, what we say to ourselves matters — a lot!

Why Self-Talk Matters

Our self-talk influences how we perceive ourselves, how we interpret events, and how we respond to challenges. When we engage in positive self-talk, we build ourselves up, boost our confidence, and cultivate a sense of resilience. On the other hand, negative self-talk can hold us back, undermine our confidence, and fuel feelings of doubt and insecurity. By becoming aware of our self-talk and learning to shift it from negative to positive, we can transform our inner dialogue and create a more empowering mindset.

Recognizing Negative Self-Talk

Now that we understand what self-talk is and why it matters, let's learn to recognize when our inner critic starts to take over. Negative self-talk often shows up as harsh or critical thoughts about ourselves, our abilities, or our circumstances. It's like a dark cloud that hangs over us, casting shadows of doubt and insecurity.

Identifying Negative Self-Talk

Here are some common examples of negative self-talk:

- "I'm not good enough."
- "I'll never be able to do this."
- "Everyone else is better than me."
- "I'm such a failure."
- "I always mess things up."

When we catch ourselves thinking these kinds of thoughts, it's important to pause and recognize them for what they are—just thoughts, not facts. By shining a light on our negative self-talk, we can begin to challenge and change it.

Flipping Negative to Positive

Now that we've identified our negative self-talk, let's learn how to flip it to positive! This doesn't mean ignoring reality or pretending everything is perfect. Instead, it's about reframing our thoughts in a more constructive and compassionate way.

The Power of Positive Affirmations

Positive affirmations are short, uplifting statements that we can repeat to ourselves to challenge negative thoughts and reinforce positive beliefs. They're like little seeds of positivity that we plant in our minds, nurturing them with love and care. Here are some examples of positive affirmations:

- "I am capable of handling whatever comes my way."
- "I believe in myself and my abilities."
- "I am worthy of love and respect."
- "I choose to focus on the good in myself and others."
- "I am proud of who I am becoming."

Using Positive Affirmations Cards

One fun way to practice positive self-talk is by using positive affirmation cards. These are small cards with uplifting messages that you can carry with you or display in your room. Each day, choose a card at random and read the affirmation aloud to yourself. Let the words sink in and allow yourself to believe them. You can also create your own affirmation cards with personalized messages that resonate with you.

Role-Playing Positive Self-Talk

Another effective way to practice positive self-talk is through role-playing. This involves acting out scenarios where positive self-talk can be applied. For example, you could pretend to be faced with a challenging task, such as giving a presentation in front of your class. Practice responding to your inner critic with positive, encouraging words like:

- "I've prepared for this, and I'm ready to shine."
- "Mistakes are a natural part of learning and growing."
- "I believe in myself, and I know I can do this."

Creating a Self-Talk Jar

To reinforce positive self-talk on a daily basis, create a "self-talk jar" filled with encouraging phrases or affirmations. Write down positive statements on strips of paper and place them in a jar or container. Each morning, reach into the jar and pull out a random affirmation. Carry it with you throughout the day as a reminder to speak kindly to yourself and challenge negative thoughts whenever they arise.

Practice Gratitude Journaling

Gratitude journaling is another powerful tool for cultivating positive self-talk and focusing on the good in our lives. Each day, take a few minutes to write down things you're grateful for, whether it's big things like family and friends or small things like a sunny day or a delicious meal. By shifting our focus to the positive aspects of our lives, we train our minds to see the beauty and abundance all around us.

How to Start Gratitude Journaling

● Set aside a few minutes each day to write in your gratitude journal, whether it's in the morning, before bed, or during a quiet moment.
● Write down three things you're grateful for each day, big or small. Try to be specific and descriptive.
● Reflect on why you're grateful for each item on your list and how it makes you feel.
● Notice how gratitude journaling shifts your perspective and brings more positivity into your life.

Conclusion

Congratulations! You've completed Chapter 4: Positive Self-Talk. We've explored the power of self-talk, learned to recognize and flip negative self-talk to positive, used positive affirmation cards for daily practice, role-played scenarios where positive self-talk can be applied, created a self-talk jar filled with encouraging phrases, and practiced gratitude journaling to focus on positive thoughts.

By embracing the magic of positive self-talk and cultivating a mindset of optimism, confidence, and self-love, you can overcome challenges with grace and resilience. Remember, the words you say to yourself matter, so choose kindness, choose positivity, and watch as your inner world transforms into a place of endless possibility and joy. Keep shining bright, my friend!

Chapter 05

Mindfulness and Being Present

Welcome to Chapter 5: Mindfulness and Being Present! In this chapter, we'll embark on a journey of exploration into the wonderful world of mindfulness. Get ready to discover the beauty of living in the present moment and learn simple yet powerful techniques to cultivate mindfulness in your everyday life.

Understanding Mindfulness

Mindfulness is the practice of paying attention to the present moment with openness, curiosity, and acceptance. It's about fully engaging with whatever we're experiencing right here, right now, without judgment or attachment to the past or future. Mindfulness helps us become more aware of our thoughts, emotions, and sensations, allowing us to respond to life's challenges with clarity and calmness.

Why Mindfulness Matters

In today's fast-paced world, it's easy to get caught up in the hustle and bustle of daily life, constantly thinking about what's next or dwelling on the past. Mindfulness offers a refuge from the chaos, allowing us to find peace and clarity amidst the noise. By practicing mindfulness, we can reduce stress, enhance focus, improve emotional regulation, and cultivate a deeper sense of connection with ourselves and others.

The 5 Senses Exercise

Let's start our mindfulness journey with a simple yet powerful exercise called the "5 senses" exercise. This exercise helps us anchor ourselves in the present moment by engaging our five senses: sight, hearing, smell, taste, and touch.

How to Do the 5 Senses Exercise

1. **Find a Quiet Space:** Sit or stand in a comfortable position in a quiet space where you won't be disturbed.
2. **Take a Deep Breath:** Close your eyes and take a few deep breaths to center yourself.
3. **Engage Your Senses:** Slowly open your eyes and take a moment to notice:

- **Sight:** What do you see around you? Notice the colors, shapes, and textures.
- **Hearing:** What do you hear? Pay attention to the sounds nearby and in the distance.
- **Smell:** What do you smell? Take a deep breath and notice any scents in the air.
- **Taste:** What do you taste? If you have a snack nearby, take a small bite and savor the flavor.
- **Touch:** What do you feel? Notice the sensations of your clothing against your skin or the texture of objects around you.

4. **Take Another Deep Breath:** Take a final deep breath and thank yourself for taking this moment to be present.

Reflecting on the Experience

After completing the 5 senses exercise, take a moment to

reflect on your experience. How did it feel to engage with each of your senses? Did you notice any changes in your thoughts or feelings? Remember, the goal of this exercise isn't to change anything—it's simply to observe and be present with whatever arises.

Mindfulness Nature Walks

One of the most beautiful ways to practice mindfulness is by taking a nature walk. Nature has a way of grounding us and connecting us to the present moment in a profound way. Whether you're strolling through a park, hiking in the mountains, or walking along the beach, pay attention to the sights, sounds, and sensations around you.

Tips for Mindful Nature Walks

- Go Slowly: Take your time and walk at a leisurely pace, allowing yourself to fully soak in the beauty of nature.

- Use Your Senses: Engage all your senses as you walk—notice the colors of the flowers, listen to the birds singing, feel the warmth of the sun on your skin.

- Stay Curious: Approach your walk with a sense of curiosity and wonder, as if you're exploring nature for the first time.

- Practice Gratitude: Take a moment to express gratitude for the natural world and all its wonders.

Guided Mindfulness Meditation for Kids

Now, let's explore a guided mindfulness meditation to help you relax and unwind. Find a comfortable position either sitting or lying down, and close your eyes if you feel comfortable doing so. Take a few deep breaths to center yourself and prepare for the meditation.

Guided Mindfulness Meditation Script

1. Body Scan: Begin by bringing your attention to your breath. Notice the sensation of the air entering and leaving your body. Take a few deep breaths, allowing each inhale to fill your lungs with fresh, revitalizing air, and each exhale to release any tension or stress.

2. Relaxing Your Body: Now, shift your focus to your body. Starting from the top of your head, slowly scan down through your body, noticing any areas of tension or discomfort. With each breath, imagine that you're sending warmth and relaxation to those areas, allowing them to soften and release.

3. Breathing Awareness: Bring your attention back to your breath. Notice the rise and fall of your chest with each inhale and exhale. Allow your breath to be your anchor, keeping you grounded in the present moment.

4. Mindful Observation: Now, bring your awareness to your surroundings. Notice any sounds around you —

the gentle rustle of leaves, the chirping of birds, or the hum of distant traffic. Allow these sounds to simply be, without needing to label or judge them.

5. Gratitude Practice: Take a moment to reflect on something you're grateful for in this moment. It could be something small, like the warmth of the sun on your skin or the beauty of nature surrounding you. Hold this feeling of gratitude in your heart for a few breaths.

6. Closing: When you're ready, slowly begin to bring your awareness back to your body and the present moment. Wiggle your fingers and toes, gently open your eyes, and take a moment to thank yourself for taking this time to practice mindfulness.

The Body Scan Technique

The body scan technique is another powerful mindfulness practice that helps us relax and release tension from different parts of our body. It involves systematically scanning through each part of the body, from head to toe, and noticing any sensations or areas of tension.

How to Do the Body Scan

1. Find a Comfortable Position: Lie down on your back in a comfortable position, with your arms by your sides and your legs slightly apart.
2. Close Your Eyes: Close your eyes and take a few deep breaths to center yourself and relax.

3. Start at the Top: Begin by bringing your attention to the top of your head. Notice any sensations or areas of tension in your scalp, forehead, and face. Take a few deep breaths to release any tension in these areas.

4. Move Downwards: Slowly scan down through your body, moving from your head to your neck, shoulders, arms, chest, abdomen, hips, legs, and feet. Notice any sensations or areas of tension in each part of your body, and breathe into those areas to release any tightness or discomfort.

5. Stay Present: As you scan through your body, try to stay present with whatever sensations arise, whether they're pleasant, unpleasant, or neutral. Remember that the goal isn't to change anything—it's simply to observe and be present with whatever is happening in your body.

Mindful Coloring Activities

Finally, let's explore mindful coloring activities as a fun and creative way to enhance focus and concentration. Mindful coloring involves coloring with intention and awareness, focusing on the present moment and the sensations of coloring.

How to Practice Mindful Coloring

1. Choose Your Coloring Materials: Select a coloring book or printable coloring pages, as well as your favorite coloring tools such as colored pencils, markers, or crayons.

2. Set the Scene: Find a quiet, comfortable space where you can focus without distractions. Create a relaxing

atmosphere with soft lighting, calming music, or a scented candle if you like.

3. Focus Your Attention: As you color, bring your attention to the sensations of coloring — the texture of the paper, the movement of your hand, the sound of the coloring tool on the page.

4. Stay Present: Notice the colors you're choosing and how they blend together on the page. Allow yourself to get lost in the process of coloring, letting go of any worries or distractions.

5. Express Yourself: There's no right or wrong way to color mindfully. Let your creativity flow and express yourself freely through color and design.

Conclusion

Congratulations! You've completed Chapter 5: Mindfulness and Being Present. We've explored the concept of mindfulness, practiced a "5 senses" exercise to engage with the present moment, used nature walks to practice mindfulness outdoors, included a guided mindfulness meditation for kids, taught the body scan technique to relax different parts of the body, and incorporated mindful coloring activities to enhance focus.

By incorporating mindfulness into your daily life, you can cultivate a deeper sense of presence, peace, and well-being. Remember, the present moment is where life unfolds, so take a deep breath, anchor yourself in the here and now, and embrace each moment with open arms. Keep shining bright, my mindful friend!

Chapter 06

Identifying and Expressing Emotions

Welcome to Chapter 6: Identifying and Expressing Emotions! In this chapter, we'll dive into the fascinating world of emotions, exploring how to recognize, understand, and express our feelings in healthy and constructive ways. Get ready to embark on a journey of self-discovery and emotional empowerment!

Understanding Emotions

Emotions are like colorful threads woven into the fabric of our lives, adding depth, richness, and meaning to our experiences. They can range from joy and excitement to sadness and anger, and everything in between. By learning to identify and express our emotions, we can cultivate greater self-awareness, strengthen our relationships, and navigate life's ups and downs with grace and resilience.

Using Emotion Cards

One helpful tool for identifying emotions is emotion cards. These are cards with pictures or words representing different emotions, allowing us to visually identify and label how we're feeling. Here are some common emotions you might find on emotion cards:

- Happy
- Sad
- Angry
- Excited
- Scared
- Surprised
- Disappointed
- Proud

Exploring the Feelings Wheel

To dive deeper into the rich tapestry of emotions, we can use a feelings wheel. This is a circular diagram that categorizes emotions into primary and secondary categories, helping us explore a wider range of feelings. Start with the basic emotions in the center of the wheel and gradually move outward to more nuanced emotions. This can help us become more attuned to our emotional landscape and better understand the complexity of our feelings.

Expressing Emotions

Once we've identified our emotions, the next step is learning how to express them in healthy and constructive ways. Suppressing or ignoring our emotions can lead to stress, anxiety, and relationship conflicts. By expressing our emotions authentically and respectfully, we can foster deeper connections with others and honor our own emotional experiences.

Teaching Appropriate Expression

It's important to teach kids that all emotions are valid and acceptable—it's how we express them that matters. Here are some tips for expressing emotions in a healthy way:

● Use "I" statements to express how you feel without blaming others (e.g., "I feel angry when you interrupt me").

- Practice active listening and empathy when others share their emotions with you.
- Take time to cool off and calm down before addressing intense emotions.
- Use nonverbal cues like facial expressions and body language to convey your feelings.

Role-Playing Emotional Scenarios

Role-playing is a fun and effective way to practice expressing emotions in different situations. Create scenarios where characters experience various emotions, and take turns acting out how they might express those emotions. This helps kids develop empathy, communication skills, and emotional intelligence.

Fostering Open Communication

Open communication is the key to creating a supportive and emotionally healthy family environment. Encourage kids to share their feelings openly and honestly, without fear of judgment or criticism. Here are some ways to foster open communication about feelings within the family:

- Schedule regular family meetings to check in and discuss how everyone is feeling.
- Create a "feelings corner" where kids can go to express their emotions through art, writing, or conversation.
- Model healthy emotional expression by sharing your own feelings and experiences with your kids.

Developing an Emotion Journal

An emotion journal is a wonderful tool for reflecting on our daily experiences and tracking our emotional highs and lows. Each day, take a few minutes to write down how you're feeling, what events or situations triggered those feelings, and how you responded to them. This can help us identify patterns, gain insights into our emotional triggers, and develop strategies for coping with difficult emotions.

How to Start an Emotion Journal

1. Choose a Journal: Find a notebook or journal that you can dedicate to your emotions. You can also use a digital journaling app if you prefer.
2. Set Aside Time: Set aside a few minutes each day to write in your emotion journal. This could be in the morning, before bed, or during a quiet moment.
3. Reflect on Your Feelings: Take a moment to reflect on how you're feeling in that moment. Use emotion cards or the feelings wheel to help you identify and label your emotions.
4. Write Freely: Write freely about your feelings, thoughts, and experiences. Don't worry about grammar or spelling—just let your emotions flow onto the page.
5. Look for Patterns: As you journal over time, look for patterns or recurring themes in your emotions. Notice any triggers or situations that tend to evoke strong feelings, and consider how you can respond to them more effectively.

Conclusion

Congratulations! You've completed Chapter 6: Identifying and Expressing Emotions. We've explored the fascinating world of emotions, used emotion cards and the feelings wheel to identify how we feel, learned to express our emotions in healthy and constructive ways, practiced through role-playing emotional scenarios, fostered open communication about feelings within the family, and developed an emotion journal to reflect on daily experiences.

By mastering the art of identifying and expressing our emotions, we can deepen our self-awareness, strengthen our relationships, and navigate life's ups and downs with grace and resilience. Remember, emotions are like colorful brushstrokes on the canvas of our lives — each one adding depth, texture, and beauty to our human experience. Keep exploring, keep expressing, and keep shining bright, my emotionally intelligent friend!

Chapter 07
Developing Empathy

Welcome to Chapter 7: Developing Empathy! In this chapter, we'll dive into the wonderful world of empathy—a superpower that allows us to understand and share the feelings of others. Get ready to explore the magic of empathy, cultivate compassion, and make the world a brighter, kinder place!

Understanding Empathy

Empathy is the ability to understand and share the feelings of others. It's like putting yourself in someone else's shoes and seeing the world through their eyes. When we practice empathy, we become more attuned to the emotions and experiences of those around us, fostering deeper connections and creating a sense of belonging.

Why Empathy Matters

Empathy is the glue that holds our relationships together, fostering understanding, compassion, and cooperation. It helps us navigate conflicts, support one another through challenges, and celebrate each other's joys and successes. By cultivating empathy, we can build a more caring and inclusive world where everyone feels seen, heard, and valued.

Learning Through Stories

One powerful way to cultivate empathy is through stories. Storybooks, movies, and videos allow us to step into the shoes of fictional characters and experience life from their perspective. Choose stories that feature diverse characters and explore themes of kindness, empathy, and understanding. After reading or watching, discuss the characters' feelings, motivations, and actions, and encourage kids to reflect on how they would feel in similar situations.

Role-Playing Empathetic Scenarios

Role-playing is another effective way to practice empathy. Create scenarios where characters experience various emotions and challenges, and take turns stepping into their shoes. Encourage kids to imagine how the characters might be feeling and to respond with empathy and compassion. This helps build empathy muscles and strengthens our ability to understand and relate to others' feelings.

Volunteering and Helping Others

One of the most powerful ways to cultivate empathy is by volunteering or helping others in our community. Whether it's volunteering at a soup kitchen, participating in a charity event, or simply lending a helping hand to a neighbor in need, acts of kindness have a ripple effect that spreads joy and compassion far and wide. Encourage kids to get involved in volunteer opportunities that align with their interests and passions, and remind them that even small acts of kindness can make a big difference in someone's life.

The Empathy Challenge

Ready for a fun and meaningful challenge? Introducing the Empathy Challenge! The goal of this challenge is to perform at least one kind act every day to show empathy and compassion towards others. Here are some ideas for empathy challenges:

- Write a thank-you note to someone who has made a difference in your life.
- Offer to help a classmate with their homework or school project.
- Compliment someone and tell them something you appreciate about them.
- Hold the door open for someone or offer to carry their bags.
- Reach out to a friend who may be feeling lonely or down and offer a listening ear.

Reflecting on Empathy

After completing the Empathy Challenge, take a moment to reflect on how showing empathy made you and others feel. Notice any changes in your own feelings and attitudes, and consider how you can continue to cultivate empathy in your daily life. Remember, empathy is like a muscle—the more you practice it, the stronger it becomes.

Conclusion

Congratulations! You've completed Chapter 7: Developing Empathy. We've explored the wonderful world of empathy, learned through stories and role-playing, encouraged kids to volunteer and help others, embarked on the Empathy Challenge, and reflected on the power of empathy to create positive change in our lives and communities.

By cultivating empathy, we can build stronger relationships, foster kindness and compassion, and create a more inclusive and caring world for all. Remember, empathy is not just something we feel—it's something we do. So let's continue to practice empathy every day, one kind act at a time, and watch as our world transforms with love and understanding. Keep shining bright, my empathetic friend!

Chapter 08

Managing Anger

Welcome to Chapter 8: Managing Anger! In this chapter, we'll explore strategies to help kids understand, express, and manage their anger in healthy and constructive ways. Get ready to tame the "anger monster" and discover the power of calming techniques to find inner peace and serenity.

Understanding Anger

Anger is a normal and natural emotion that everyone experiences from time to time. It's like a warning sign that something isn't right and needs attention. However, anger can sometimes feel overwhelming and out of control, leading to conflicts and challenges in our relationships. By learning to understand and manage our anger, we can transform it from a destructive force into a constructive tool for growth and self-awareness.

The Anger Iceberg

Imagine an iceberg floating in the ocean. What you see above the surface is just the tip of the iceberg—visible anger that others can see and hear. But beneath the surface lies a vast expanse of hidden feelings and emotions that fuel our anger. This is known as the "anger iceberg." By exploring the deeper layers of our anger, we can uncover the underlying emotions and needs driving our reactions, such as hurt, frustration, fear, or sadness.

Anger Management Strategies

Now that we understand the complexity of anger, let's explore some practical strategies for managing it effectively.

Counting to Ten

When we feel anger bubbling up inside us, it's important to take a pause before reacting. One simple technique is counting to ten slowly in your head. This gives us time to cool off and think before we speak or act, allowing us to respond more calmly and rationally to the situation.

Taking a Time-Out

Sometimes, the best way to manage anger is to step away from the situation for a while. Taking a time-out gives us space to calm down and collect our thoughts before addressing the issue. Find a quiet place where you can relax and unwind, whether it's a cozy corner in your room or a peaceful spot outdoors.

Visualizing the Anger Monster

The "anger monster" activity is a fun and creative way to visualize and tame anger. Draw or create a picture of an anger monster, giving it a name and a personality. When you feel angry, imagine the anger monster stirring inside you, and visualize yourself taming it with calming techniques like deep breathing or positive self-talk.

Creating an Anger Plan

An anger plan is like a roadmap for managing anger effectively. Sit down with your child and create a personalized anger plan with steps to follow when they feel angry. This could include strategies like:

- Recognizing the warning signs of anger (e.g., clenched fists, racing heart).
- Taking deep breaths to calm down.
- Counting to ten or taking a time-out.
- Talking to a trusted adult or friend about their feelings.
- Engaging in a favorite activity to distract themselves from anger.

Releasing Anger Energy

Physical activity is a great way to release pent-up anger energy in a healthy way. Encourage kids to engage in activities like jumping jacks, running, dancing, or punching a pillow to release tension and frustration. By channeling their energy into physical movement, they can calm their minds and bodies and regain a sense of balance and control.

Creating a Calm Corner

A calm corner is a designated space in your home where kids can go to relax and unwind when they're feeling angry or upset. Fill the calm corner with calming items like:

- Soft pillows or cushions to sit or lie on.
- Fidget toys or stress balls to squeeze and manipulate.
- Favorite books or calming music to soothe the mind.
- Sensory items like kinetic sand or textured objects to explore.

Conclusion

Congratulations! You've completed Chapter 8: Managing Anger. We've explored strategies for understanding, expressing, and managing anger in healthy and constructive ways, including the anger iceberg, counting to ten, taking a time-out, visualizing the anger monster, creating an anger plan, releasing anger energy through physical activities, and developing a calm corner at home.

By mastering the art of anger management, kids can learn to navigate their emotions with grace and resilience, transforming anger into an opportunity for growth and self-discovery. Remember, anger is a powerful emotion, but it doesn't have to control us. With patience, practice, and the right tools, we can learn to tame the "anger monster" and find inner peace and serenity. Keep shining bright, my calm and composed friend!

Chapter 09

Building Resilience

Welcome to Chapter 9: Building Resilience! In this chapter, we'll embark on a transformative journey to discover the power of resilience—the ability to bounce back from challenges and adversity stronger than before. Together, we'll explore the keys to cultivating resilience in kids, empowering them to navigate life's twists and turns with courage, confidence, and inner strength.

Understanding Resilience

Resilience is like a sturdy ship navigating stormy seas— it helps us weather life's challenges and emerge stronger and more resilient than before. At its core, resilience is the ability to adapt, persevere, and thrive in the face of adversity, setbacks, and obstacles. Resilient individuals possess a sense of inner strength, optimism, and hope that allows them to rise above adversity and find meaning and purpose in difficult times.

The Importance of Resilience

Resilience is not just about bouncing back from adversity—it's about bouncing forward, using challenges as opportunities for growth and transformation. Resilient individuals are better equipped to cope with stress, overcome obstacles, and navigate life's ups and downs with grace and resilience. By cultivating resilience, kids can develop the skills and mindset needed to face life's challenges with confidence, courage, and resilience.

Learning Through Stories

Stories have the power to inspire, uplift, and empower us to overcome obstacles and achieve our dreams. Whether it's books, movies, or real-life examples, stories can teach valuable lessons about resilience and perseverance. Choose stories that feature resilient characters who face adversity with courage, perseverance, and resilience. After reading or watching, discuss the challenges the characters faced, how they overcame them, and the lessons they learned along the way.

Examples of Resilient Characters

- Harry Potter: Despite facing numerous challenges and setbacks, Harry Potter demonstrates courage, resilience, and a willingness to stand up for what is right.
- Moana: Moana embarks on a journey of self-discovery and resilience as she navigates treacherous waters and confronts powerful adversaries to save her people.
- Malala Yousafzai: Malala's inspiring story of resilience and courage in the face of adversity serves as a powerful reminder of the importance of standing up for what you believe in, even in the most difficult circumstances.

Practicing Problem-Solving

Problem-solving is a key skill for building resilience. By approaching challenges with a positive attitude and a can-do mindset, kids can learn to overcome obstacles and find creative solutions to problems. Practice problem-solving through fun games and puzzles that challenge kids to think critically, brainstorm ideas, and work together as a team. Encourage a growth mindset by celebrating effort, persistence, and creativity, rather than just focusing on the end result.

Problem-Solving Activities

- Puzzle Challenges: Solve puzzles or brain teasers as a family, encouraging kids to think outside the box and experiment with different problem-solving strategies.
- Scavenger Hunts: Organize scavenger hunts that require kids to solve clues and navigate obstacles to reach the treasure, fostering teamwork and critical thinking skills.
- STEM Projects: Engage in STEM (Science, Technology, Engineering, and Mathematics) projects that encourage kids to design, build, and problem-solve their way to solutions.

Using Resilience Reminders

Resilience reminders are like little seeds of inspiration that nourish our resilience and inner strength. They can take the form of quotes, affirmations, or drawings that remind us to stay strong, keep going, and never give up, even in the face of adversity. Display resilience reminders in visible places like the refrigerator, bathroom mirror, or bedroom wall, where kids can see them regularly and draw strength from their positive messages.

Examples of Resilience Reminders

- "You are stronger than you know."
- "Every setback is a setup for a comeback."
- "When life knocks you down, get back up stronger."
- "You've got this!"
- "Believe in yourself and anything is possible."

Developing a Resilience Routine

A resilience routine is a set of daily practices and activities that help kids build resilience and inner strength. Create a family routine that includes resilience-building activities such as:

- Daily Gratitude Practice: Take a moment each day to reflect on three things you're grateful for, fostering a positive mindset and appreciation for life's blessings.
- Mindfulness Meditation: Practice deep breathing and mindfulness exercises to calm the mind and reduce stress, promoting emotional resilience and well-being.
- Physical Activity: Engage in regular exercise or outdoor play to boost mood and energy levels, promoting physical and mental resilience.
- Journaling: Write down your thoughts, feelings, and

experiences to gain insights and perspective, fostering self-awareness and emotional resilience.

- Family Bonding Time: Spend quality time together as a family, sharing stories, laughter, and love, strengthening bonds and fostering emotional resilience.

Conclusion

Congratulations! You've completed Chapter 9: Building Resilience. We've explored the power of resilience, learned through stories and problem-solving activities, used resilience reminders to nourish our inner strength, and developed a resilience routine to cultivate resilience and well-being in our daily lives.

By building resilience, kids can develop the skills and mindset needed to overcome challenges, thrive in the face of adversity, and live life with courage, confidence, and resilience. Remember, resilience is not just about bouncing back — it's about bouncing forward, stronger and more resilient than before. Keep shining bright, my resilient friend!

Chapter 10

Creating a Balanced Routine

Welcome to Chapter 10: Creating a Balanced Routine! In this chapter, we'll explore the importance of establishing a balanced daily routine for kids. A well-rounded routine helps children thrive by providing structure, stability, and opportunities for growth and development. Let's dive in and discover how to create a balanced routine that promotes health, happiness, and success.

Understanding the Importance of Balance

A balanced routine is like a carefully orchestrated symphony—it harmonizes different aspects of life to create a melody of well-being and fulfillment. Balance is key to maintaining physical health, emotional well-being, and academic success. By establishing a balanced routine, kids can cultivate healthy habits, manage their time effectively, and achieve a sense of harmony and equilibrium in their daily lives.

The Benefits of Balance

- Promotes Health and Wellness: A balanced routine ensures that kids get enough sleep, exercise, and nutritious food, supporting their physical health and well-being.
- Fosters Emotional Well-Being: Regular routines provide a sense of stability and predictability, reducing stress and anxiety and promoting emotional resilience.
- Enhances Academic Performance: A well-rounded routine includes time for homework, study, and enrichment activities, helping kids excel

academically and reach their full potential.

- Strengthens Family Bonds: Family time is an essential component of a balanced routine, fostering strong relationships, communication, and support.

Components of a Balanced Routine

A balanced routine encompasses various activities and responsibilities, including schoolwork, play, rest, and family time. Here's how to incorporate these components into your child's daily schedule:

Schoolwork:

- Allocate specific time slots for homework, study, and school-related activities.
- Break tasks into manageable chunks and prioritize assignments based on deadlines and importance.
- Create a designated study area free from distractions to promote focus and concentration.

Play:

- Schedule time for unstructured play and creative activities.
- Encourage outdoor play to promote physical activity, exploration, and imagination.
- Provide a variety of toys, games, and materials to inspire creativity and curiosity.

Rest:

- Establish consistent bedtimes and wake-up times to ensure adequate sleep.
- Create a relaxing bedtime routine with activities like reading, taking a warm bath, or practicing relaxation techniques.
- Limit screen time before bed and create a calm, soothing sleep environment.

Family Time:

- Set aside dedicated time each day for family activities and bonding.
- Plan fun outings, game nights, or shared meals to connect and strengthen family bonds.
- Use family meetings to discuss schedules, goals, and upcoming events.

Teaching Time Management Skills

Time management is a critical skill for success in school and life. Teach kids how to manage their time effectively by:

- Making a simple schedule or to-do list to organize tasks and prioritize activities.
- Breaking tasks into smaller, manageable steps and setting realistic goals.
- Using timers or alarms to stay on track and manage time efficiently.
- Encouraging independence and self-directed

learning by allowing kids to manage their own schedules and deadlines.

Promoting Healthy Habits

A balanced routine also includes activities that promote physical health and well-being. Encourage regular physical activity and healthy eating habits by:

- Incorporating daily exercise into your child's routine, such as walking, biking, or playing sports.
- Providing nutritious meals and snacks that include a variety of fruits, vegetables, whole grains, and lean proteins.
- Teaching kids about the importance of hydration and encouraging them to drink plenty of water throughout the day.

Adjusting the Routine

Flexibility is key to maintaining a balanced routine. Use a weekly check-in to assess how well the routine is working and make adjustments as needed. Encourage open communication and collaboration to ensure that the routine meets your child's needs and preferences.

Weekly Check-In:

- Sit down with your child at the end of each week to review the routine and discuss what worked well and what could be improved.
- Encourage your child to share their thoughts,

feelings, and suggestions for making the routine more effective and enjoyable.

- Use feedback from the check-in to make any necessary adjustments to the routine and set goals for the upcoming week.

Conclusion

Congratulations! You've completed Chapter 10: Creating a Balanced Routine. We've explored the importance of establishing a balanced daily routine for kids, including time for schoolwork, play, rest, and family time. By creating a well-rounded routine, kids can cultivate healthy habits, manage their time effectively, and achieve a sense of harmony and equilibrium in their daily lives. Remember, balance is the key to health, happiness, and success. Keep shining bright, my balanced friend!

CONCLUSION

Congratulations, young explorers! You've reached the end of our journey through "Emotional Intelligence and Self-Regulation for Kids Ages 6–10." As we bid farewell, let's take a moment to reflect on the valuable lessons and empowering strategies we've discovered along the way.

Recap of Key Points and Strategies

Throughout this book, we've delved into the fascinating world of emotional intelligence and self-regulation, exploring:

- Understanding Emotions: Identifying and expressing our feelings through storytelling and role-playing.
- Recognizing Stress: Using tools like the stress thermometer and relaxation techniques to manage stress.
- Deep Breathing Techniques: Harnessing the power of breath to calm the mind and body.
- Positive Self-Talk: Flipping negative thoughts into positive affirmations and practicing gratitude.
- Mindfulness and Being Present: Engaging our senses to cultivate mindfulness and focus.
- Building Empathy: Understanding and sharing the feelings of others through stories and role-playing.
- Managing Anger: Taming the "anger monster" and developing healthy coping strategies.
- Building Resilience: Bouncing back from challenges with courage, optimism, and perseverance.
- Creating a Balanced Routine: Establishing a well-rounded schedule that promotes health, happiness, and success.

Continuing the Journey

As you continue on your journey, remember that emotional intelligence is a lifelong skill that can be honed and refined over time. Keep practicing the strategies you've learned, and don't be afraid to ask for help or support when needed. Your family and friends are here to cheer you on every step of the way!

A Message of Motivation

Dear young adventurers, always remember that life is a grand adventure filled with twists, turns, and unexpected surprises. Embrace each challenge as an opportunity for growth and self-discovery. You are capable, resilient, and full of infinite potential. Keep shining your light bright, and never forget the incredible impact you can have on the world around you.

Thank You and Keep Sharing!

Thank you for joining us on this journey of self-discovery and growth. We're so proud of all you've accomplished and the progress you've made. Keep sharing your stories, experiences, and progress with others—you never know who you might inspire along the way.

Until we meet again, may your hearts be filled with love, your minds with curiosity, and your spirits with boundless joy. Keep shining, my dear friends, and may your journey be filled with endless adventures and discoveries!

With warmest wishes,

Dalton Wyman

Made in United States
Troutdale, OR
01/11/2025

27854764R00046